PATRIOTIC SYMBOLS

The Liberty Bell

Nancy Harris

Heinemann Library
Chicago, Illinois

Customer Service **888-454-2279**

Visit our Web site at **www.heinemannlibrary.com**

Photo research by Tracy Cummins and Heather Mauldin
Designed by Kimberly R. Miracle
Maps by Mapping Specialists, Ltd.
Printed and bound in China by South China Printing Company

10 09 08 07
10 9 8 7 6 5 4 3 2 1

10 Digit ISBN: 1-4034-9381-2 (hc)   1-4034-9388-X (pb)

Library of Congress Cataloging-in-Publication Data
Harris, Nancy, 1956-
  The Liberty Bell / Nancy Harris.
    p. cm. -- (Patriotic symbols)
  Includes bibliographical references and index.
  ISBN 978-1-4034-9381-1 (hc) -- ISBN 978-1-4034-9388-0 (pb) 1. Liberty Bell--Juvenile literature. 2. Philadelphia (Pa.)--Buildings, structures, etc.--Juvenile literature. 3. Signs and symbols--United States--Juvenile literature. I. Title.
  F158.8.I3H37 2007
  974.8'11--dc22
                            2006039377

Acknowledgements
The author and publisher are grateful to the following for permission to reproduce copyright material: ©Alamy **p. 16** (North Wind Picture Archives); ©Corbis **p. 5** (flag, Royalty Free), **8, 11** (Bob Krist), **14** (Bettmann), **15** (Bettmann), **17** (Francis G. Mayer), **19** (T.E. Marr), **20** (Bob Krist), **22** (Bob Krist), **23** (Bob Krist); ©Getty Images **pp. 5** (quarter, Don Farrall), **6** (Francesco Ruggeri), **10** (Tom Gralish), **21** (Wayne Eastep); ©The Granger Collection **p. 12**, ©istockphoto **pp. 4** (drbueller), **23** (drbueller); ©Shutterstock **pp. 5** (Statue of Liberty, Ilja Mašík), **5** (White House, Uli); ©SuperStock **pp. 9, 13**.

Cover image reproduced with permission of ©SuperStock (age fotostock). Back cover image reproduced with permission of ©istockphoto (drbueller).

Contents

What Is a Symbol?

The Liberty Bell is a symbol.
A symbol is a type of sign.

A symbol shows you something.

A symbol can have words.

The Liberty Bell

The Liberty Bell is a special symbol.

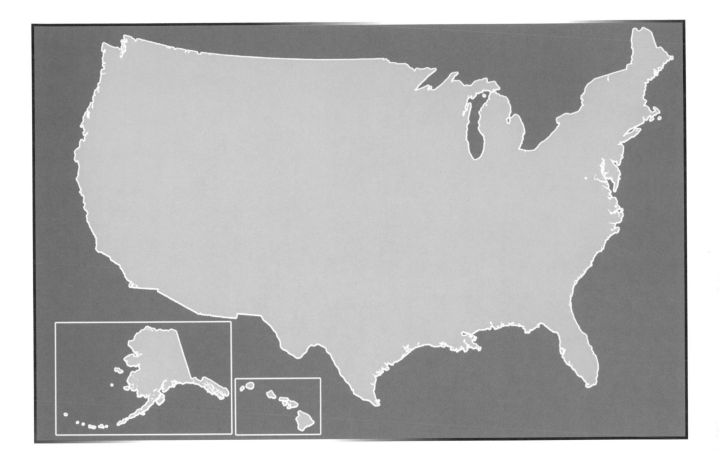

It is a symbol of the United States of America.
The United States of America is a country.

The Liberty Bell is a patriotic symbol.

It shows the beliefs of the United States.
The bell ringing is a symbol of freedom.

Words

Special words are on the Liberty Bell.

The words tell us the people are free.

Pennsylvania

The Liberty Bell hangs in Pennsylvania.
It was first rung there.

It was a symbol of freedom.
The freedom was for the people living there.

The people decided how they would live.

The people made laws.
The laws were rules people followed.

The people were proud of their freedom.
They rang the bell to honor their freedom.

The people worked together.
They worked to make Pennsylvania strong.

The United States of America

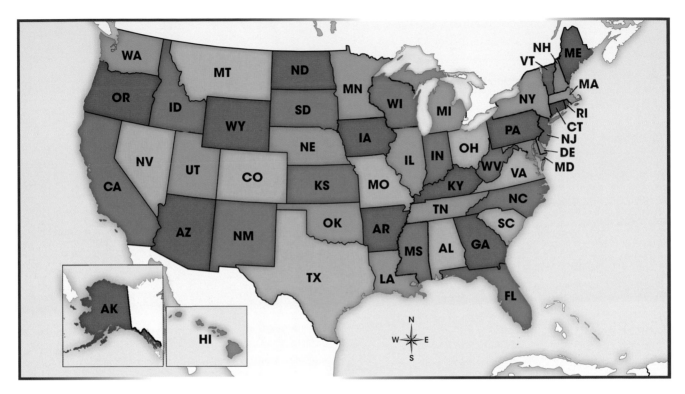

The bell is now a symbol for the United States of America.

It is a symbol of freedom for all the people in the country.

What It Tells You

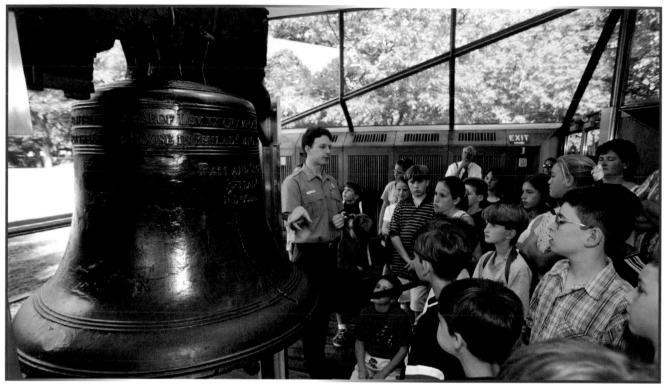

The bell reminds people of their freedom.

They are free to live as they choose.

Liberty Bell Facts

★ The Liberty Bell was first called the State House Bell.

★ The Liberty Bell has a large crack in its side.

Timeline

1700   1750   1752   1800

✪ The Liberty Bell was made in 1752.

Picture Glossary

country an area of land that is ruled by the same leader

patriotic believing in your country

symbol something that stands for something else. Symbols can stand for feelings, places, or objects.

Index

Note to Parents and Teachers

The study of patriotic symbols introduces young readers to our country's government and history. Books in this series begin by defining a symbol before focusing on the history and significance of a specific patriotic symbol. Use the timeline and facts section on page 22 to introduce readers to these non-fiction features.

The text has been carefully chosen with the advice of a literacy expert to enable beginning readers success while reading independently or with moderate support. An expert in the field of early childhood social studies curriculum was consulted to provide interesting and appropriate content.

You can support children's nonfiction literacy skills by helping students use the table of contents, headings, picture glossary, and index.